SET FREE

From The Grip of Grief, Bitterness, Anger, Hatred, and Unforgiveness by the Power of Love

RACHEL THOMPSON

Published by Rachel Thompson in Partnership with
Bold Publishing (https://boldpublishings.com)

Book Design by Opeyemi Ikuborije

Manufactured in the United States of America

ISBN: 979-8-9917255-8-3

Library of Congress Control Number: 2025906751

Follow Rachel Thompson

Social Media Outlets:

Facebook: Rachel Thompson
Instagram: Setfree115
LinkedIn: Rachel Thompson
TikTok: @Setfree115

CONTENTS

Dedication

First of all, I would like to dedicate this book to my mom, Raisola Harrien Bryant, whom I love so dearly. I dedicate this book to her because she lost her life trying to protect mine (in a sense). Also, because when she was here with us, she taught me how to love, and I found out that the Scripture is true in my life. "Love never fails." It was the love that she taught me and left with me that brought me through and **SET me FREE.**

Second, I dedicate this book to my husband Vester Thompson Jr., who has partnered with me in changing the lives of many for the Kingdom of God.

I dedicate this book to my three sons, Terry Hathorn, Mikell Hathorn and Zachary Thompson, my daughter-in-law Candi Hathorn, and my two daughters Patronia and Patrinia Thompson. Remember, the Love of God will never fail you.

I dedicate this book to my three younger siblings Rosa Bridges, Lydia Mikel, and Charles Bryant (Charlie Boy). I dedicate this book to them because when our mother was so tragically killed, the younger siblings were all three under 9 years old, the youngest, Rosa was 6 years old. I always wanted and desired the very best for them. Even though Lydia (Ann) and Charles are gone from this side, I will never stop loving them. Thanks to Rosa who works alongside me as a sister and as a sister in Christ at our Church, The House of Refuge. Love has never failed us.

I dedicate this book in honor of my big brother Leon who was a pillar for the family until his sudden passing away shortly after my mom was killed. He was only around 18 years old when my mom was killed.

This book is also dedicated to all the people who are experiencing pain from the violent loss of a parent. It is dedicated to all those who feel that they can't be set free from the torment of the tragedy. It is dedicated to all those who have been broken through tragedy and trauma, and are in need of restoration and healing.

It is also dedicated to: those who are desiring to be made whole again; those who feel trapped and hopeless, because of trauma and tragedy; the women who feel trapped in an abusive relationship, and have remained in it, afraid that they can't survive outside of that abusive relationship; those who struggle with letting go of anger, unforgiveness, hatred and bitterness towards those who have caused the tragedy and trauma to come into their lives. This book is to educate, encourage, and show them how to let it go, and that they can love through the love of God, and be **SET FREE.**

Acknowledgement

I give thanks and honor first of all to my Heavenly Father who has healed and set me free from the grip of grief, bitterness, pain, anger, unforgiveness, hatred and confusion. I thank You Lord for inspiring and directing me to write this book as a healing tool, so that many others can be healed and set free from the grip of these same destructive things. Without His healing my broken heart, and leading and guiding me, this book would never have been possible.

To my faithful husband and pastor, Vester Thompson, who has supported and loved me unconditionally and has encouraged me in every way as I have taken this challenge to write this book. Thank you for your ever-loving support—spiritual, physical, and financial; not only in writing this book but in life as we have journeyed together.

To Mikell Hathorn and Zachary Thompson, thank you for honoring and supporting me. Although you both have faced many challenges in life, you have persevered and have been a great support to me, during this process. Special Thanks to you and all of our children, Terry and Candi Hathorn, Patronia and Patrinia Thompson. Thank you for supporting me in every way. (Proverbs 31:28 KJV) says, "Her children arise up, and call her blessed…"

Special thanks to my sister Rosa Bridges who has supported me in my journey in many ways. You have been there for me— working and taking some of the load off me, so that I can write and expand in ministry. Thank you for your willingness to partner with me in all that the Lord set at my hands to do.

A special thanks to my sisters Annette Harrien and Helen Ruth Reese, who gave up their homes and careers in other states to come and live in the family home with us after my mom was killed. Thanks to you; we did not have to go into a foster home. Thanks for doing your best.

Thanks to my two oldest sisters, Irma Louise Newsome, and Arlene Siler, who took in my younger siblings for periods of time after my mom was killed. Thanks to you for taking on the responsibility of handling services, arrangements and other things after the tragedy happened; when everything was so chaotic and we were so confused. Thank you.

Special thanks to my writing coach and CEO of Bold Publishing Company, Dr. Denise Nicholson who ministered to me as I poured out my story. Thanks for the encouragement and direction. Thanks for your compassion, patience, and commitment to the mission. Thank you for the Writing Incubator challenge. It has been a blessing to me. Thank you for helping me to unleash the story that was on the inside of me. Thanks to you and your entire team at Bold Publishing.

Special thanks to the House of Refuge intl. Church family. Thanks for your motivation and support.

Special thanks to Cyris J. Jones, the author of "Thank God for what you have; Trust God for What you Need." Thank you, Cyris, for being a great encouragement to me in my writing process. Thanks for helping me to get connected to a great writing community of writers.

Special thanks to Dr. Shanicka N. Scarbrough, MD and Elder Lorece White, who both have been an encouragement to me as we have ministered the healing Word together—to the family and others. Thank you both for encouraging me to write this book. The great books that you both have written have been a great inspiration and encouragement—proving that we can do all things through Christ who strengthens us.

Finally, I would like to give special thanks to the Kenneth Copeland Ministry and the Victory Channel, with which we have been partners for over 10 years. Thanks for the continuous prayers and encouragement on behalf of your partners. Thank you both: Brother Kenneth and Sister Gloria Copeland.

Foreword
By Les Brown

You have something special.

You have greatness within you.

And you've been chosen to do the **Greater Work**.

Every so often, a book comes along that doesn't just inform, it transforms. *Set Free from the Grip of Grief* by Rachel Thompson is that kind of book.

Rachel takes you by the hand and walks you through the valley of grief with grace, wisdom, and authenticity. With deep compassion and powerful storytelling, she reminds us all that while grief may grip us, it doesn't have to define us.

This book is more than words on a page. It's a heartfelt journey that leads you from the darkness of sorrow and bitterness into the healing light of love and forgiveness. Rachel's insights are a beacon for those who feel lost in their pain, and her courage will inspire you to find your own.

She shows us that healing is possible. That love is the greatest force for transformation. And that inside each of us is the power to release anger, embrace peace, and live again with hope.

If you're holding this book, I believe it didn't find you by accident.
You're ready to be set free.
You're ready to rise.
And you're ready to walk into your next chapter, stronger, and lighter, by the power of love.
Read this book with an open heart. Let it do its work in you.
And then share it, because someone else you know needs it too.

You've got greatness within you. And now, it's your time.

Les Brown
Motivational Speaker, Author, and Coach

Preface

Romans 15:13 – May the God of hope fill you with all joy and peace as you trust in Him, so that you may overflow with hope by the power of the Holy Spirit. This scripture has been stirring in my spirit, and as I read Set Free, I was filled with awe at how one can endure such devastating circumstances and still break free from the bondage of hopelessness. Over the years, I have watched many believers in Christ become trapped in a cycle of feeling lost, confused, bitter, hurt, and angry over the painful experiences in their lives.

There are two types of survivors: those who succumb to their pain, sinking deeper into the destructive nature of sin, and those who overcome, flourishing in the abundant life given by Christ Jesus. The key difference? Those who live victoriously, fully healed, are the ones EMPOWERED by the Holy Spirit—fueled with hope for a better future. This empowerment comes from trusting the Lord with all our hearts, refusing to rely on our own understanding of our circumstances.

Pastor Rachel is no exception to this truth. The Word of God, planted as a seed in her heart as a young, abused child, took root in her darkest hour: the tragic loss of her mother at the hands of her father. When bitterness threatened to take hold and bear the fruit of destruction, it was the power of LOVE—an echo of her mother's heart and words that severed those roots, allowing God's Word to flourish in her. From conception, Rachel was on the enemy's radar. Yet, the Lord's hand covered and protected her in the midst of her pain and turmoil. Her story is one of redemption, forgiveness, and the unfathomable love of God that brings peace beyond understanding. In it, we witness the supernatural power of God to heal, deliver, and SET FREE.

May this testimony of Jesus be a prophecy in your own life, declaring that what He has done before, He desires to do it again—for you.

Shanicka Scarbrough, MD
Author of Power to Heal Your Heart
www.DrShanicka.org

Introduction

This story is a journey through pain, bitterness, grief, hatred, and unforgiveness. The day my father killed my mother, it felt like the ground beneath my feet shattered; nothing would ever be the same. Just a few days before my father killed my mother we were walking—my mother and I—in the field—not far from our house. She seemed to have had something very heavy on her mind. She had her hands behind her back and I was right behind her. We were not in conversation—just walking. All of a sudden, my father emerged from the edge of the woods and pointed his rifle toward us. I immediately fell to the ground in fear of him. My mom looked down at me and said, "Gal get up from there, your daddy is not going to hurt you." So, I got up and clung onto her as I stood behind her. She didn't really think that he would do to her what he did just a few days later. With the very same rifle, he took her life, leaving me devastated. Because of the trauma and tragedy that I have experienced, and the healing that I have received from and through the Love of God, I wanted to share with others, that there is healing and deliverance available for them, and for all those who have suffered the loss of a parent through violence, even at the hand of the other parent.

For all those who are dealing with the spirit of grief, anger, bitterness, unforgiveness, hatred, and confusion; for all those who can't seem to get past the hurt and the pain and even the shame of that tragic event in their lives, this book is for you. This book is also to enlighten those who are in abusive relationships of the danger and destruction that it poses to them and their entire family. I hope this book will encourage them to seek help; healing is for them. We must remember that, it's not what we have experienced in life, but it is how we navigate through it. This book will help readers navigate through anger, grief, hatred, and devastation after a tragic loss of a parent or other loved one, and guide them to truths as to how to let go and forgive. Perhaps you have gone through betrayal, are heartbroken from a relationship, or have been hurt by the actions of others and are in need of letting go of the anger, bitterness, hatred, and unforgiveness.

This book is also a healing tool for you. Your journey to healing, deliverance, victory, and freedom starts here. Claim it!

"If the Son sets you free, you will be free indeed" (John 8:36 NIV).

CHAPTER 1

The Aftermath of Violence

FINDING OUT

On the 26th of February, when I was 13 years old, I left home and went to school as usual. It was a Tuesday, early afternoon; my oldest brother Leon came to the school to pick up my sister and I at the junior high school campus. I was puzzled as to why he was picking us up so early. He said that Mama was sick. I tried to imagine what could have happened to her since we left for school earlier that morning. I was thinking that she was fine that morning. Leon drove us to the emergency room entrance parking.

He backed up so that we could see the ambulance when it came. I was in the back seat. We saw the ambulance coming, but it was moving really slowly. Leon began to exclaim with an 'oh no' attitude, "Mama is dead y'all, Mama is dead!" The driver parked the ambulance, got out and looked towards us as we were still in the car and he dropped his head and shook it to say, "She is gone." When he did that, my world shattered around me. I grabbed my head and I screamed as loud as I could, "No-o-o!" I couldn't believe that what he indicated was true. At that time, I didn't know what had happened—why she was dead. My brother drove us home, the hearse was backed up under the carport, and they were bringing her body out of the house.

"Oh no, this is true." That's when I found out that Daddy had Killed Mama. He had come in through the back door and shot her in the back. She fell at the door. Everyone was in shock, fear and anger. We were in unbelief that this had actually happened. I remember as my mom's body was being put in the hearse, a lady sat me down on the front porch and ministered to me in the middle of all the confusion. I don't remember what she said to me, but I remember that she just ministered love and compassion to me. I had never seen her before but I do remember her telling me that her father was a preacher. She was driving a Cadillac. I will never forget what she did for me and I don't remember ever seeing her again. At that time, I was in pieces: mentally, confused, full of anger, and questioning, "Why?"

During all that time I learned that my younger siblings were gotten off the bus across the highway at the neighbor's driveway, because the police had everything blocked off. My youngest sister Rosa, told me that they would not let them come home because of what had happened. It was chaotic!

The house was filled with people—some familiar, some strangers. The air felt heavy: the day was strange and gloomy. I was hurting, alone, and angry. I had been separated from the most important person in my life. You see, I always called myself a mama's baby. I was incredibly close to her, always by her side while my siblings were off doing other things. I would dream of growing up, getting a job, and buying her all the things she wanted but couldn't afford.

That night, after the tragedy, I remember hearing my youngest sister, Rosa, crying out, "Mama, mama." Her voice was filled with sadness and confusion, as if she were asking, *Mama, where are you?* I felt so broken, so helpless. I couldn't bring Mama back for her. I couldn't comfort her. For all of us, it was a day of mournful tears and unbearable anguish. My mom's sisters were in rage. My oldest sister on my mom's side was angry. She had left home as a teenager and went to live with my aunt because of the abuse of my father. I kept asking why he did such a thing and why was he so mean and evil?

I found out that my father shot her in the back and let her lay there for a long period of time, and later went and told the neighbors, "I think that I have killed Ras." He later broke the rifle in two and waited for the police. He was arrested and went to jail, though he never served any prison time. There we were left without a mother or a father.

My mom went to work in the afternoons and worked the night shift in a neighboring town. I found out that she was getting ready to go to work and Daddy came in through the back door. I believe that he surprised her. This time she saw that he was really going to do what he had been threatening to do all those years. He often would tell her that he was going to kill her. She was running towards the door—running for her life when he shot her in the back and she fell face down at the door.

She was at home alone; When my oldest brother, Leon was at home Daddy would not hurt my mom. At the time Leon was around 18 years old and just finishing High school. Daddy didn't like Leon very much. That is why my dad waited until mama was alone.

All I could visualize was her running for her life. I could hear her in my mind saying, "Willie no!" I could visualize her falling to the floor. I thought about how she must have felt when she was laying there on the floor before she died. It appeared that she didn't die immediately. Those thoughts and many others haunted me for years. And to worsen the trauma, we had to live in the same house where the tragedy happened.

Living there was a daily reminder of the incident as the years went by. There was no respite. I found out that my father had rejected God. When you reject God, you make everyone around you miserable. He had totally surrendered to walk into the generational curses that were handed down to him. You see, his father was a cruel man. I was told two things concerning my dad's mom's death. I was told by my father that she was a full-blood Indian and my grandfather was the slave master's grandson.

I was told that my paternal grandmother, Lula, was pushed off a high back porch by my grandfather; my father's father, and later died. She fell sick and grandpa refused to go and get the doctor right away. Grandpa waited days until she was dead before he went and got the doctor, and by then it was too late. Her body was put on a thing called a cooling board (in those days) and she lay there in the house on that until they buried her body. I was told by my aunt that they cut off long plaits of grandma Lula's hair and gave it to each of the girls. Mama left 10 children that she had birthed. My dad's mom left 10 children. The oldest was about 16, about the age of my father's oldest son by my mom. The youngest one was somewhere about six to eight years old. My youngest sibling was six years old at the time. These are the kind of evil things that happen in families when they surrender to generational curses. It causes pain.

The impact of my mom's death was broad. It shook my mom's parents' world too. My mom was very close to her parents. She helped them both a lot. She really helped my grandpa a lot because he was, for the most part, blind. For the family a daughter and sister's life had been taken. To her grandchildren, their grandmother was suddenly gone. Lynn, her eldest biological grandchild, was old enough to understand the painful truth, her grandmother's life had been taken. The six grandchildren by marriage, who also lovingly called her Grandma Ras and were deeply loved in return, felt the same heartbreaking loss. To all the nieces and nephews whom she knew so well on her side of the family, to them Aunt Ras's life had been taken so suddenly. To the neighbors, friends, fellow church members, co-workers her life had been taken and it was a shocker to our community. Things were never the same.

There was much darkness and upset on that day. I saw the world through a different lens when I found out what had happened that day. The love, the hate, the bitterness, anger, numbness and confusion overwhelmed me. I was devastated. The question was, "Where do I go from here in my life without my mom?"

Tips and Tools:

What questions are you asking right now?

- Write them down.
- Ask God for the answers.
- Listen for them (the answers).

Notes

CHAPTER 2

The Weight Of Anger

March 3, was my mom's funeral at the church where she grew up. It was an awful day for me, and that day just happened to be my birthday. I remember my next to oldest sister taking us a few days before to buy my sisters and I new outfits to wear to the funeral. My sister, next to me, and I bought dresses that were alike, except that one was purple and the other was pink. Mine was the purple one. It had ruffles around the neck and around the waist. I wore that dress that day, but I don't think I wore it ever again. That day was the day I realized that my mother really would not be coming back—never again. Back to life as usual, back to being Mama.

I went up to view my mother's body during the funeral and I thought, *This is my mama*. I touched her forehead and it was so cold and hard. I screamed and cried so hard. That touch sent me into another world, I was so angry with my daddy for doing this final act of violence to my mom. I realized that she could never come back home. I was devastated. Anger began to manifest itself, but not outwardly. It was brewing on the inside. Anger brewed inside as each day went by. I daily replayed what my dad had done, how he killed Mom. I cried daily. I missed my mom. I remember the following spring, I went out in the front yard and dug a large flower bed in the shape of my mom's first initial, which was

R. Everything I did was centered around grief and missing my mom. The hatred grew deeper for my dad.

I lost interest in school. I had no one to hold me accountable for my school work and grades, so I didn't care anymore. I did some mischievous things as a teenager, but I was reminded that mama didn't train me that way. I wanted to be a bad girl, but I couldn't. Thank God!

My two older sisters moved back home from other states where they had been living. They came to live with us. They were very young and lived their lives. I am so glad that the hand of God was upon my life from birth.

Anger and grief were killing me little by little. You see, I had been living with an angry father every day. The resentment and hatred started long before that dreadful day that he took Mom's life. My dad would drink until he was down drunk. He would cuss and call Mama really ugly names. He would do a lot of that cussing at night after everyone had gone to bed but we still could hear him fussing and cussing. He would often get his gun and we would have to run up through the loft and even out of the house at night in the dark. It was horrible. At one point he burned one side of my mom's face with a hot iron. Another time he hit her on her leg with a thick glass soda bottle and broke the vessels in her leg. It was a really bad area on her leg, which never went away. He would give her black eyes pretty often and she would wear a scarf to try and hide them. I would see her put cream on her face daily for years trying to fade the burned spots. The scars never completely went away.

He would often tell her, "I'm going to kill you." I remember asking my mom one day, "Why don't you leave daddy?" When he would do evil, she would tell us, "Love your daddy." Well, I didn't want to love him. Mama told me that she was staying because she didn't want, in her words, to have her little children strewn up and down the road. In other words, she didn't have anywhere to go. I understood that she had left daddy at one point, but her father, whom she loved and respected so much, sent her back home to her husband. So, I suppose that she felt trapped, having nowhere else to go.

Hatred for him was growing on the inside of me not only because of what he was doing to my mom, but also how he treated us children with cruelty. The day my dad committed that heinous crime— taking my mom's life, just made what was brewing on the inside of me heighten to a level of bitter hatred. Here I was angry, bitter, full of grief, hatred, and unforgiveness. There was a day that it was arranged for us as children to go to visit him at the facility where he was. We—my siblings and I were driven there. They brought him outside to spend time with us.

My other siblings were communicating with him but I couldn't. How and why did he want to see us and spend time with us? I didn't want anything to do with him. I hated him with a passion. I stayed away from him. I wanted harm to come to him. All of this was building up on the inside of me but God kept me in the midst of this destructive hatred.

The Bible says to be angry and sin not. To get angry at sin or wrongdoing is not an unnatural response, but anger should not become who you are. Anger was becoming who I was in a sense. I hated to think about him, his name, or anything that had to do with him. I thank God that He delivered me from the spirits of anger, hatred, bitterness, and grief. I was being tormented every day. I dreamed about my mom, basically every night. Sometimes I dreamed that we would find her in an old car under some old clothes or in an old house, only to wake up and find out that she was not there. This went on for years. On top of all that, I found out that my father murdered my mom and he would serve no prison time. He was advised by an official that his trial was coming up and that he should leave the state, and he did. He never served any prison time. This on top of the anger, bitterness, resentment, and the hatred that was already there was huge. He took my mom's life. He took her away from me. I was missing my mom, grieving for her and was full of hatred, and bitterness toward him. All of this was killing me. I felt like I was going to lose my mind. I felt like I was going to explode: holding all those 'explosives' inside. This went on for many years. I didn't feel that I had anyone to turn to, as I dealt with the hatred and anger toward my father—anyone that I could pour out to. So, I just kept it all stored up inside. I grew up as a shy little girl. As I was dealing with those "explosives" I could hear my mom's voice in my head saying, "Love your daddy." I learned that Love (God) never fails. I said to the Lord, "I can't love him."

One day I cried out to the Lord, "Lord, I can't take this anymore!" I was at my breaking point. That night, the Lord showed me my mother in a dream. She was in this huge field of flowers. She was sitting down with all of her children around her. Even though at the time most of the children had reached adulthood, we were all young children in the dream. We were leaning on and around her lap. Everything was so bright and beautiful. She expressed to all of us, "I love y'all but where I am, I don't want to come back." I woke up. I was FREE! To know that my mom was in a place where she didn't want to come back to her little children whom she loved so much, had to be a beautiful place. I knew that she was with the Lord. The Lord had **set me free**. I felt like a different person. The weight of hatred and grief had been lifted. I was dying, and bleeding on the inside. Hatred, anger and bitterness were indeed destroying me.

During this cleansing process, the Lord showed me that my mom was with Him. My dad could have gotten forgiveness and accepted the Lord and they both could be in heaven. My dad was still alive at the time. I came to the realization that I could have died with that hatred, anger, and bitterness in my heart and gone to hell; even though I didn't pull the trigger that killed my mom. I later was able to love my dad. The Lord showed me, "No, you can't love your dad by yourself, but in Me you can love him." And I did. I was even able to lay hands on my dad and he received healing. I was also able to minister to my mom's siblings concerning him. My dad told my husband and me that he had his business fixed. I had to get to the point of realizing that I could not handle that crisis on my own. The hatred, anger, bitterness and grief were too much for a natural man to bear. It was toxic and explosive. If I had not turned to the Lord and cried out to Him for help, I believe that I would have been consumed with it to the point of losing my very life and soul.

The weight of the anger was heavy. I had the opportunity years later to minister to some of my mom's siblings concerning forgiveness towards my father as well. That's what happens when The Lord delivers you. You will want to see others set free as well. Anger is a divider; it separates families. The weight of anger, unforgiveness and bitterness is heavy. I was a very bitter person, although one could not tell from looking at me on the outside. The Bible says that anger rests in the bosom of fools. The Savior tells us to come unto Him if we are heavy laden and that He will give us rest.

Tips and Tools:

I felt angry, confused, bitter, unforgiving, grief, and hatred.

I felt like I had nowhere to turn for help.

I felt like I was about to lose my mind.

What are you feeling right now?

Write it down.

You are not alone. Many of us have felt anger, resentment, deep bitterness, unforgiveness, and hatred towards those who have hurt us. If you are having any of those feelings, healing, deliverance, and freedom are possible for you. It is not a sin to get angry, but you don't want to die under the weight of it. The curse stops here. Break the cycle! Hurt people, hurt people. Let it go!

Scriptures references

"Be ye angry, and sin not: let not the sun go down upon your wrath" (Ephesians 4:26 KJV).

"Looking diligently lest any man fail of the grace of God; lest any root of bitterness springing up trouble you, and thereby many be defiled" (Hebrews 12:15).

"And when you stand praying, if you hold anything against anyone, forgive them, so that your Father in heaven may forgive you your sins" (Mark 11:25).

"And forgive us our debts, as we forgive our debtors" (Matthew 6:12).

"Surely, He hath borne our griefs and carried our sorrows…" (Isaiah 53:4).

Notes

_____
_____
_____
_____
_____
_____
_____
_____
_____
_____
_____
_____
_____
_____
_____
_____
_____
_____
_____
_____
_____
_____
_____
_____

CHAPTER 3

Finding a Path to Healing

My pathway to healing began as I stated in chapter two, when I came to the realization that the burdens of grief, unforgiveness, bitterness and anger were too much for me to handle on my own. I realized that I was dying from the inside out and couldn't get control of it. My pathway to healing began when I came to myself, like the prodigal son who came to himself when he was in the hog pen. He realized that he was going to die if he didn't get back to the care of His father who had more than enough to help him.

The Prodigal son realized that he couldn't do it on his own. He had to surrender his ways to his father's ways. He was in the hog pen, and I was in a pit. A pit filled with disappointments, hatred, bitterness, confusion, desperation and unforgiveness. I realized that the hatred that I had for my dad was poisoning me. The Lord shook me and showed me that I was allowing the evil acts that my dad committed towards my mom and the family, to put me on a path to my own destruction. The Lord also showed me that my dad could get forgiveness. God allowed me to see that His will is for all to be saved and that He would "in no wise" turn away those who come to him, no matter what they have done.

I then realized that I was guilty of sin myself. I was guilty of breaking the greatest commandments of all, and that was to love my neighbor as myself. My mother kept reminding me to love my daddy. Love (God) never fails. It does not matter how bad the situation, healing is possible through God. Love was the pathway to healing when I made the decision to come out of that dark pit. Remember, life is full of decisions.

If we don't make the right decisions, we could sink deeper and deeper into the pits of despair, hopelessness, and torment . Yes, I thought that my dad deserved to die or at least be punished for what he had done to us all, but I had to realize that the love that mama talked about would not fail me if I would open myself up to allow it to operate through me. I realized just how heavy the grief was and how it was tormenting me. I could feel that the problem and weight were growing bigger and getting heavier by the day. Each day more grief, bitterness, anger, hatred, and unforgiveness were added to the load. It was indeed destroying me. When I realized that I was heading for destruction I could go no further down that road. I cried out for help and that's when the pathway to healing opened up for me, and I began to walk in the Love that my mama talked about—the Love (God)that never fails. I began to recognize that this love walk was a supernatural thing. I had to admit to the Lord and to myself that I really couldn't love my dad. I had to confess that I didn't want to love him either. I couldn't love him. Love and unforgiveness cannot work together in the same heart.

When I confessed my inability to love my dad, the Lord made me aware that it would not be me, the natural man that would be doing the loving; I should just surrender, let go, and allow Him to Love my dad through me—I would just be the conduit. The Lord said to me, "No, you can't love him, but through Me you can." That is what sent me down my pathway to healing and freedom. I then understood that healing was possible for me. I began to think Love. The Lord asked, "If you had the opportunity to see harm, evil or destruction come upon your dad, would it be a good feeling to you in your inner man? My answer was,

"No, I don't want to rejoice to see him suffer. At that moment I realized that healing was being manifested to my broken heart. I then began to feel love and compassion toward my dad.

My dad drank alcohol, and had chronic hiccups. The Lord told me one day to go get my dad and take him to my house; lay hands on his throat, and pray for him. I obeyed and did as the Lord had said and he was healed instantly. He went back and told his drinking buddies and they asked if they could get prayer. Wow! It was then that I knew that God had brought me out of that horrible pit. At one point I didn't want him anywhere near me. Now, I was laying healing hands on him.

If you have been hurt and your heart has been hardened and you have become bitter toward someone who has hurt you— perhaps a parent, a sibling or maybe it is your spouse who betrayed you, or someone else close to you. I want to say to you, healing is possible for you. Deny your feelings and take on the love walk that only Jesus can take you on. Love Never fails. First you must admit to the Lord your inability to love and forgive. You must realize and admit that you have a problem. Acknowledge the fact that you can't love or forgive by yourself, but through God you can. Healing is possible for you, and Love never fails. My mom preached love, as I have often said. She even preached love from 'the grave', and it (Love) never ever failed me. Love will yield peace if you keep your mind stayed on Him (God).

We must realize that, oftentimes the person who hurts us was hurt somewhere in his or her life. It could go back to some past pain and trauma that were never healed or resolved. However, this does not excuse their bad actions towards you. Confess that the curse stops here and that healing is possible for you (me) today. People like you and me deal with issues coming at them from many directions, and no matter how it may affect other people, Love (God) never fails.

Healing is a process and must be a continued effort on your part. No one can get your healing for you. Remember that Joseph was put in a pit; it was not his decision, but the prodigal son put himself in the hog pen because of his bad decision. I felt justified by putting myself in that dark pit full of bitterness and hatred—I didn't think I could let it go. I felt that I could never come out of that dark pit. I chose to hold on to the hurt and the pain. Then I had to let it go. You must let it go!

What are you feeling right now concerning that person that you don't feel you can forgive? Healing and forgiveness are possible for you. You are not the only one who has been hurt or betrayed and feel that this pit of unforgiveness is too deep for you to climb out of. Just remember that, with God all things are possible.

"But With men this is impossible; but with God all things are possible" (Matthew 19:26).

"He sent His word, and healed them, and delivered them from their destruction" (Psalm 107:20).

Tips and tools

Do you feel bitter towards someone who has caused you pain?

Write down why you feel bitter and release it, let it go.

Notes

_____

_____

_____

_____

_____

_____

_____

_____

_____

_____

_____

_____

_____

_____

_____

_____

_____

_____

_____

_____

_____

_____

_____

_____

CHAPTER 4

Rebuilding Family Bonds After Tragedy

"And they that shall be of thee shall build the old waste places: thou shalt raise up the foundations of many generations; and thou shalt be called, The repairer of the breach, The restorer of paths to dwell in" (Isaiah 58:12 KJV).

The night after my mom was killed, I couldn't go to sleep. I could hear my six-year-old baby sister's little voice crying out, "Mama, Mama." My heart was so broken to hear her crying for Mama, and I couldn't help her. It was a night of unrest, sorrow, and confusion. The question in my mind was, *where do we go from here without our mother.* We were orphans. My mom was close to her mother, her father, and her siblings. We often went to Grandma and Papa's house. My mom was a great asset to her parents. She honored and respected them and did whatever she could to help them. When that tragic event happened, it made a big tear in our family unit.

Ras, as many called my mom, was gunned down so brutally. Everyone knew about the abuse, but no one really ministered to the need. No one thought that this would actually happen. It was a slap to everyone, even our community. No one was saying anything good about my dad at that time. So, it was a time of anger and questions. "Why did he do this?" This was coming from my older siblings, my mom's family and the community. When my aunts referred to my dad, they didn't have good things to say about him at all, and I understood their feelings. After all, that was their sister.

When tragedy happens, it is important to be able to administer love and forgiveness in the situation even though this might be very difficult. The thing that is promoted the most in a crisis will affect those involved for years down the road—whether that be negative or positive. As the years went by, my three younger siblings went to live with my oldest sister in California, where my dad was. They spent time with him; even after spending that time with my dad, my second youngest sister never got over what he had done.

I was just thirteen years old when Mama was killed. My sister was only fifteen, and my brother was around sixteen or seventeen. The three of us were left in our parents' home, trying to navigate life without the structure and security we had always known. My oldest brother Leon, who found my mom's body, was there as well. At the time Leon was around 18 years old and just finishing high school. He soon moved to the Gulf Coast for employment. To add to the grief, Leon suddenly passed away just a few years after mama was killed. We all loved Leon very much, He was our big brother who gave us some form of protection. He was suddenly gone.

Though our two adult sisters returned from New Jersey and California with their families to care for us, the household became chaotic. We deeply missed the order and discipline our mother had instilled in us. Before she died, we had everything we needed; now, we struggled with instability, hard times and loss.

Years later, one of my aunts confided in me that she had wanted to take me in but couldn't bear the thought of separating us. *Wow,* I thought. I wished she had stepped in anyway. Looking back, I longed for the guidance and support I so desperately needed during that time.

How do you rebuild after a storm, when you are still wrestling through the aftermath of the storm. Sometimes the big storms leave behind many little storms of life to battle. The question is, how do you rebuild? "And they that shall be of thee shall build the old waste places..." (Isaiah 58:12)

Rebuilding after a storm, in the case of a tragedy such as mine required hard work. It required a massive cleanup. The pieces had to be scooped up and gathered up, and I had to figure out what was usable and what was not. In these kinds of *purging* we must replace the old, damaged, or ruined with the new; repairing that which is usable and discarding that which is not. This process can be painful—letting go of that which is not usable in our lives anymore. We had the memories, but I had to come to the realization that I couldn't rebuild on memories alone. When rebuilding a family, picking up the pieces, you may want it back the way it was before, but then you must realize that is not possible.

I thank God that He allowed me to see and feel His hand upon my life even after the big storm and in the midst of the little storms that sprung up from the big storm. Jesus told His disciples to pick up the fragments after he had fed the multitude with the little boy's lunch which consisted of two fish and five barley loaves. After Jesus gave thanks and blessed the little boy's lunch, it fed the multitude and there were 12 baskets of fragments left. When they were filled, He said unto His disciples, "Gather up the fragments that remain, that nothing be lost" (John 6:12).

Jesus told His disciples to pick up the fragments. There was life in the fragments. They were not whole fish and loaves, but because they had been blessed, there was life sustaining substance in the pieces. How do you rebuild? First, pick up the pieces. How do you rebuild in the midst of the mini storms spun off of the big storm? You keep moving. Don't quit, and don't stop.

Some of the mini storms in my life were deep poverty, despair, unforgiveness, anger, hopelessness, hunger, low self-esteem, and lack in many areas.

Parents are the *parenthesis* around the family. One of the mini storms that I experienced was the lack of the *parenthesis*—no protection, no boundaries. I remember in the midst of all these storms. However, I never stopped dreaming, and hoping for a brighter day.

One of the pieces of my life that was no longer usable was the love of my mother's presence. I loved her so much. As a little girl I dreamed and confessed that when I grew up and got a job I would lavish my mom with all the lovely things that I would buy for her. I felt like she deserved it. But when I picked up that piece, I saw that it was no longer usable and I had to discard it. I couldn't hold on to it.

Though I was fighting through all these mini storms, I still dreamed of coming out of that dark pit, although I didn't know how at that time. I still wanted better for my three younger siblings. I would say to myself, *When I get grown, I am going to Put my family back together. I was going to get my younger siblings, Rose, Ann, and Charlie Boy.* I was dreaming of rebuilding. I felt like that was the least that I could do for my mom. I felt like I owed it to her. They were in different places at various times—Chicago, California, Louisiana and Mississippi. How do you rebuild in this case? You can only rebuild, if you work with that which is usable and discard that which is no longer usable.

I remember this particular mini storm: One Thanksgiving after my mom was killed, someone had given my older sister a turkey. At that time, we didn't have food, running water, gas, or electricity. However, we did have a fireplace. So, my sister cooked the turkey on the fireplace in a pan or pot the night before. She left it on the fireplace overnight. When we got up the next morning, we realized that the rats, yes, the rats, had eaten Thanksgiving dinner first. I thank God that I can look back now and laugh instead of crying. My sister cut off the parts where the rats had eaten from and we ate the rest.

Yes! We ate it! That's all we had to eat. Even in the midst of all of this, I never stopped dreaming—dreaming and hoping for a brighter day. That was a part of the rebuilding.

Another mini storm that I remember well is that one of my sisters and I wore the same clothes. We had very few clothes. I would wear my set of clothes one day and my sister would wear them the next day. We would swap up. That was all we had.

On top of all that, while we were trying to rebuild, one of my sisters' best friends told her that her grandmother, who was a leader in the community church where we had attended, said to her concerning us, "They are not going to be nothing." Wow! I never forgot those words.

How do you rebuild? **Be determined to beat the odds**. When I heard those words, I was determined to come out of that temporary mini storm of poverty and lack. I was determined that I would be something, and I kept on dreaming in the midst of the storms.

Healing and rebuilding is possible for you. The same Love that my mama talked about, the love that never fails was in those pieces that I picked up. Many times, I would steal away to read my Bible and pray, even though I didn't understand what and why I was going through, what I was going through.

I always had this tugging to know the Lord, even when my mom was alive. I didn't talk about it because I didn't understand it. I thought that I was different and abnormal. After my mom was killed, some of my siblings would catch me in hiding, reading my Bible and would make fun of me. They would call me Miss Nun. That didn't feel good at the time, but I realize now that reading the Bible was giving me strength.

What big storm have you been in and how many mini storms have spun off in your life? I encourage you to analyze the pieces and fragments and see what's usable and what needs to be discarded, and begin your rebuilding project. Remember, Love never fails and restoration is possible.

"And they that shall be of thee shall build the old waste places" (Isaiah 58:12 KJV).

All of those mini storms helped me to be compassionate towards others and also helped me to give freely and come to the rescue of others.

Never stop dreaming and expecting changes for the better. Don't stop in the midst of the storm. Keep moving. "For I know the plans I have for you," declares the LORD, "plans to prosper you and not to harm you, plans to give you hope and a future" (Jeremiah 29:11).

Discard the things that are no longer possible. Don't hold on to relationships, desires, etc. that are not usable anymore. If you do you will find yourself stuck and the rebuilding incomplete.

The day eventually came when I was able to go and get my two younger sisters, Rosa and Ann. I was able to bring them to where I lived. By that time, they were teenagers but I kept the dream alive. At that time my baby brother Charlie was out of my reach. During the course of time the Lord enabled me to come together with Rosa, Ann, and eventually Charlie Boy, to pour into their lives. They have been a blessing to me. Ann, who is deceased, came back to me about 3 years before she passed away and I was able to minister forgiveness to her concerning our dad. She had never gotten over what he had done.

After all those years, she was still bleeding on the inside. One of her mini storms was that she overheard two older sisters talking after our mom was killed. She overheard them talking about who was going to take her and who was going to take Rosa. She said to me, "Rachel, neither one of them wanted me, they both wanted Rosa. They didn't want me!" She was so hurt by that, and she kept it inside all those years. I ministered healing to her soul.

- I was able to also minister the Word to Charlie who recently passed away. We became quite close before he passed. He would come to church with us and I saw him pretty often. Rosa is and has been a vital part of our Church ministry. We work in ministry together. She is a blessing and I get to pour into her life constantly. I still remember her little voice crying out that horrible night, and I couldn't help her. Thanks be to God, now I can. He helped us to rebuild the old waste places. Thank you God!

Tips and tools:

- Find the fragments from the storm that are usable and write them down.

- Find the fragments that you need to discard. Write them down and release them.

Notes

_____
_____
_____
_____
_____
_____
_____
_____
_____
_____
_____
_____
_____
_____
_____
_____
_____
_____
_____
_____
_____
_____
_____
_____
_____

CHAPTER 5

"Letting Go Of The Blame And Let God"

"For we are not fighting against flesh-and-blood enemies, but against evil rulers and authorities of the unseen world, against mighty powers in this dark world, and against evil spirits in the heavenly places" (Ephesians 6:12 NLT).

Blame just simply means to find fault with the imperfections and flaws of others. When we go back to the beginning, we see where Adam and Eve sinned against the commandment of God. Adam said, "That woman that you gave to be with me…". To paraphrase: "God, It's Your fault for giving me this woman so blessed and beautiful, and I could not resist".

Eve said, "The serpent, he beguiled me." (He tricked me with his subtlety, smooth talk, and persuasion).

When it all boiled down, it was the devil that was at the root of it all. They were not dealing with flesh and blood enemies, but against evil rulers and authorities of the unseen world—against mighty powers in this dark world, and against evil spirits in the heavenly places.

I say all of this to say that, all the hatred, bitterness, anger, grief, confusion, and frustration are not the results of things coming from flesh and blood (people—in particular, my dad), but it was the wicked one (Satan) that was influencing my dad to do all those cruel things that he did. My dad made bad choices with his loyalty.

I reflect on my life as a child and young adult and can recall some of the villainy that was used by the devil to scar my life.

I recall one day when my siblings and I had worked in the field, picking cucumbers, which was a big industry in the south. When we had finished for the day, my dad took the cucumbers to the vat, where they sorted, weighed, and paid my dad for them. My dad never usually promised us anything for working in the field, but that particular day, he did. He promised us ice cream. When he returned, we were so excited and were expecting to eat ice cream. Well, when my dad got out of the truck, we noticed that he was drunk. It was not unusual for him to be drunk; however, he did have the ice cream. He got out of the truck and began cursing and ranting. He took the ice cream which was a one-half gallon box of Neapolitan and threw it to the ground while we watched. *Oh no!* I thought. He then trampled on it with his foot, crushed it in the dirt, and just walked away. When he was out of sight, we hurriedly fell to the ground where the ice cream was, scraped away the dirt and ate what was left with our hands.

One might say, how could a father bring children into the world and treat them so cruelly? It goes back to the fact that we were not wrestling against flesh and blood. That was not my dad in operation; it was the wicked one in operation. My dad was just a yielded vessel.

I remember another of the many incidents: This particular time, my mom was at work, as aforestated in a prior chapter she worked at night. We had just gotten our very first telephone. It was mounted on the wall in the hallway and had a long cord. I had called my friend and was trying to keep my dad from finding out. Well, he found out. Oh, I was laughing with my friend on the phone and apparently my dad must have heard the laughter and became enraged. My sister and I at high speed disappeared into our bedroom. My sister went out the window, and I hid in the closet. The closet was a wide closet with sliding doors. I hid in the left side of the closet. The bedroom door burst open, and my dad stormed in. I could see the axe swinging. He had the axe! I froze. I stayed real still, hoping that he wouldn't see or hear me. I could see him walk over to the window because it was open. I guess he thought that my sister and I both escaped out the window. He left the window open. Whew! I was petrified; and as soon as he left the room, I slipped out of the closet, scrambled to the window and leaped out. My sister and I scampered in the dark down to a nearby bridge and stayed until we felt that it was safe to go home.

What would make a man want to do those things to his own children.? He was mean. We lived in fear! In hindsight I have discovered that we were not wrestling with a mere man, but against spiritual wickedness, and against evil powers (demons), which my dad had allowed in. In the book of Genesis, God warned Cain even before he killed his own brother, that sin was lying at his door. It is sin's desire to rule over you. When a person allows sin to rule over him/her as my dad did many times, he/she will do the will of what and who is ruling over him/her. Satan, the author of sin, is the perpetrator.

When you boil it all down, the devil and his demons were to blame. He planned to destroy the whole family in one shot. My dad was the conduit like the serpent was to Satan who brought the temptation to Eve, to disobey God. The devil's plan is to kill, steal, and destroy.

Another incident that I remember as a child was when we were at the old house where we lived. My sister, one of my brothers, and I were standing in the front room of that house. My dad got his rifle and shot toward us. The bullet flew right over my brother's head and left the bullet hole in the wall. Demons were in control.

Listen to this one: I was in the field working and my dad became angry with me while in the field. He jumped in his truck and chased me as I fled for my life on foot. Whew! I was so scared that he was going to catch up with me. These are just a few of the episodes of my life.

Although I went through some difficult and traumatic experiences, a few of my older siblings suffered even more severe abuse. What we each endured was painful in its own way, but some of their stories were especially heartbreaking. What would cause a dad to do these kinds of things to his own children? Remember, we wrestle not against flesh and blood. It is a spiritual battle.

So, when I released the blame (and all the evils that came with it) and let God have it, I came to the realization that everything and everyone that God made is good; the enemy of our souls is evil.

I had to look beyond the man and realize that this was not who we were wrestling with. I had to understand that there was a soul inside of my dad that needed saving, in spite of his wicked, inhumane behaviors.

"Wherefore henceforth know we no man after the flesh: yea, though we have known Christ after the flesh, yet now henceforth know we him no more" (2 Corinthians 5:16 KJV) "For I know that in me (that is, in my flesh,) dwelleth no good thing: for to will is present with me; but how to perform that which is good I find not" (Romans 7:18). Then, and only then can we let go of the blame (the fault of the person) and let God be God in our lives.

Blame and its evil associates will cause strife, and strife will hinder your deliverance, blessing, healing, prosperity and success. Many illnesses and diseases stem from hatred, regret, anger, resentment, and unforgiveness. Some Sicknesses and diseases start in the mind. It starts with the negative things that are being meditated on.

Proverbs 23:7 KJV says, "For as he thinketh in his heart, so is he."

How do you think with your heart? When you meditate on certain negative thoughts long enough, they will get down in your heart and take root.

What are you thinking right now toward that person who has hurt you or betrayed your trust? Are you thinking that if he /she or they had not done this to me, I would not be here in this place? Are you thinking of revenge?

Let go and pick up the pieces. You are not the only one who has had to pick up the pieces and press forward in spite of the pain. Bring those broken pieces to the Lord. He is good at healing broken hearts, broken minds, broken relationships, and broken lives.

"Finally, brethren, whatsoever things are true, whatsoever things are honest, whatsoever things are just, whatsoever things are pure, whatsoever things are lovely, whatsoever things are of good report; if there be any virtue, and if there be any praise, think on these things" (Philippians 4:8 KJV)

"Casting down imaginations, and every high thing that exalteth itself against the knowledge of God, and bringing into captivity every thought to the obedience of Christ…" (2 Corinthians 10:5 KJV).

When the thoughts of what that person did to you invade your mind (even though the person may be at fault, cast it down, in Jesus' name, and bring them into captivity (capture the bad thought) and bring them into the obedience of the Word. Command them to obey the Word. You have the Power.

We are three-part beings which are spirit, soul, and body. We are first of all, spirit, which connects to God and wants to communicate with Him. Your spirit is the real you. Secondly, we possess a soul, which deals with mind, will, and emotions. Third, we live in a body. Feed your spirit and let it be in control, not the soulish part of your being. If your soul (emotions, will, likes or dislikes) is in control, you will be living a rollercoaster life. The real you will be out of control. The soul doesn't want to love if it has been hurt. The spirit part of our being is the part that says, "I love you, even though you have hurt me, because that is the will of God."

You must grow in the Word of God: Feed on the Word; read the Word of God; meditate on the Word as you are being taught the Word; and Journal as God gives you revelation for your life. It is important to write down what God reveals to you. This will remind you of what God has spoken to you.

This commitment of walking in your healing, deliverance, and victory is not a one-time fix, it is a continuous journey, but a good journey.

Remember the Scripture says in Phil 4:13 "I can do all things through Christ who strengthens me". Yes, you can do it, but only in Christ! If your soul takes control, you will be out of control. Your soul deals with your thoughts, will, and your emotions. Emotions are not stable. Your soul will tell you that you can't forgive, you can't love, and you can't do this or that.

The soulish area of your being deals with your likes and dislikes; whether it be food, colognes, colors, or style etc. David said, "Bless the Lord oh my soul, and all that is within me, bless His holy name." David commanded his soul to comply with his spirit. David's spirit man rose up! The body has to go where your spirit and soul lead it.

You make the decision to tell yourself, "I can and I will come out of this dark place of hatred, anger, bitterness, unforgiveness, and confusion.

Forgiveness and healing are a journey. Forgiveness is an action word. Forgiveness is not just words that you speak to someone who has caused your pain, heartache or trouble.

- Forgiveness is a decision and choice that you have to make.
- Forgiveness is a cleanser. When we choose to forgive, it cleanses.
- Forgiveness is releasing the person, the pain and the hurt.
- Forgiveness is a healer. It heals the body, soul, and spirit. It brings total and complete healing.
- Unforgiveness breeds uncleanliness. It causes us to hold on to the person, the pain, and the hurt. It imprisons us in the past. It is like drinking poison expecting the one who hurts us to die.
- Unforgiveness scars the one who won't forgive, thus leaving scar tissues which can cause irritation.
- Unforgiveness can cause sickness in body and mind.

In order to come out of that pit/dungeon I had to be reminded that vengeance belongs to the Lord, and not to me. He said that He will repay. God knows how to repay.

Yes, it is right that justice be served to those who commit crimes, and I had to realize that even if my dad had served time in prison or even been given the death penalty, I still would have had to forgive him, because I was not the judge nor the jury. Vengeance belongs to God. My dad's penalty would not have released me from having to forgive him.

Do you find yourself in conflict, or arguing with people who are not even in your presence?

Do you find yourself saying: *If he/she or they had not done this or that I would have had a better life or opportunities etc. I wouldn't be unhappy or living with my heart crushed?*

Do you find yourself saying. *I wouldn't be stuck in life and not able to move forward had it not been for what this individual did or didn't do?*. You are not alone. You are not the only one who feels stuck, or trapped by this evil spirit, called unforgiveness. You can forgive through Christ. Forgiveness is by faith like everything else. The just shall live by faith. There is no other way.

Many people have been and many still are stuck at the places where they were hurt. If you are at that place, you don't have to stay there and die. Healing and deliverance are possible for you. Please take your mind off the bitter poison of revenge. Revenge will only make things worse. Ask the Lord to minister a spirit of forgiveness to you and grant you inner healing. With the help of God, begin practicing forgiveness and release that other person, in Jesus' name.

Proverbs 18:21 says, "Death and life are in the power of the tongue, and they that love it shall eat the fruit thereof." Begin every morning, confessing with your mouth:

"I forgive all those who have trespassed against me and all those who have wronged and caused me pain." Understand that when you start to declare this confession and even days and months after, you probably won't feel any different in your emotions. Regardless of how you feel in the natural, remember changes are taking place in the spiritual—little by little—day by day.

Mark 11:23 says, "For verily I say unto you, that whosoever shall say unto this mountain, 'Be thou removed, and be thou cast into the sea,' and shall not doubt in his heart, but shall believe that those things which he saith shall come to pass, he shall have whatsoever he saith." Confessions are so important to this process.

Hebrews 11:2 says, "Through faith we understand that the worlds were framed by the Word of God, so that things which are seen were not made of things which do appear."

Stop the curse. My dad walked in the curse by his own choice.

"I call heaven and earth to record this day against you, that I have set before you life and death, blessing and cursing: therefore, choose life, that both thou and thy seed may live" (Deuteronomy 30:19).

Stop the curse. Choose life. I did!

Tips and tools:

- Make the decision to forgive.
- Ask God to cleanse you.
- Ask God to help you to release that person who hurt you.
- Embrace the healing that comes from forgiveness.

Notes

_____
_____
_____
_____
_____
_____
_____
_____
_____
_____
_____
_____
_____
_____
_____
_____
_____
_____
_____
_____
_____
_____
_____
_____
_____

CHAPTER 6

Finding Purpose in Pain

"...and who knoweth whether thou art come to the kingdom for such a time as this?" (Esther 4:14 KJV).

Esther is one example of **Finding Purpose in Pain**. Sometimes we must be reminded by others that there is purpose even in our pain. Mordecai had to bring Esther into a reality check, by letting her know she was there in that position for a purpose. And if she didn't allow her purpose to come forth (in spite of the trial) God would raise up someone else to carry out that assignment.

You see, in this story of Queen Esther, we find that she had been an orphan. Her mother and her father were both brutally killed. She had been raised by her cousin, Mordecai. Mordecai loved Esther and was there encouraging and giving her godly directions.

"For if thou altogether holdest thy peace at this time, then shall there enlargement and deliverance arise to the Jews from another place. But thou and thy father's house shall be destroyed; and who knoweth whether thou art come to the Kingdom for such a time as this?" (Esther 4:14).

You see, Esther was chosen, but her background was hidden. I, likewise hid my story when grown and got my deliverance from the grief, heartache, hatred, unforgiveness, and bitterness I harbored. Yes, I hid my story.

When my husband and I got married, I had not shared my childhood life with him or anyone else. I didn't talk about it. I just wanted to be normal. I didn't want anyone to know what and where I came from— the abuse, the hatred, bitterness, and unforgiveness. I didn't want anyone to know that my dad had killed my mom. I was glad to be out of all the hardship and pain.

I thought to myself, *Let's not talk about it, ever.* I was ashamed of my past—such poverty and tragedy. I had a job and could buy little things which had been a luxury before that. As a teenager (after my mom was killed), I was determined that I would not be taken advantage of by the boys or men. I was closed up as far as relationships were concerned. My walls were built up because I was an orphan. I knew they would think that I was vulnerable.

I remember, not long after my mom's death, a grown man who visited my adult siblings asked them if he could take me for a ride, and sadly they answered, yes. Thank God that I was able to say, "No, I am not going anywhere with you." I had no *parenthesis* around me as Esther had. I thank God that I had His wisdom on the inside of me; although at that time I didn't know that's what it was.

At that time, there was a lot of partying, drinking, and even marijuana smoking at my mom's house. I told myself I wanted to join in; I thought I should—but the desire never came. Instead, I felt like something was wrong with me for not wanting to indulge. Deep down, I was always afraid that if I did, something bad would happen to me. I was timid, struggling with low self-esteem, and felt like an outsider in my own home.

This book is a book about forgiveness and releasing—releasing the hurt, pain, disappointments, hatred, bitterness and anger. This book highlights the love of God which never fails; how love brought me through the hard places and out of the dark pit. This book is about the seed of love that was sown in my life at an early age by my mom as she taught me, always saying, " Love your daddy."

I didn't want anyone to know where I had come from. But, *who knows if God had called me and preserved my life for such a time as this.* There was purpose in my pain. I kept all of the horrific things that I had experienced shut up behind iron doors until I went with my husband to a men's conference, and I heard the speaker say that he was going to share a testimony that he had not shared before. To me it was like he was going to open this door and we would see what was locked up behind those doors. When he said that and began to share, I saw those huge iron doors swing open in a vision. I had hidden all my pain— unforgiveness, bitter anger, hatred, brokenness along with poverty and lack behind those iron doors. I never wanted them to be exposed until that day when the doors swung open, and I couldn't keep them shut any longer. When I began to share my stories with my husband, Vester, he began to weep. He encouraged me to tell my testimony more, so that more people could be set free from some of those same things.

Tips and tools

What's hidden behind the iron doors in your life that's supposed to be revealed?

Write them down and release them, so God can use you to bring about healing to others.

Notes

CHAPTER 7

Preserved for the Purpose

In this chapter I share how God kept me through the pain for the purpose. We all have assignments in spite of the pain. I will share how even from the womb the hand of the Lord was upon my life.

When I was a child, my mom told me that she had the mumps when she was pregnant with me. I didn't know why she was telling me that, for I was just a child. However, I will never forget it. Years after she was killed her words kept coming back to me concerning that. Then the Lord prompted me to do some research concerning pregnant women who had come down with the mumps. I found out that pregnant women who came down with the mumps were more likely to lose their babies. I suppose that the Lord wanted me to be aware of His love for me and that His hand was upon me even from the womb. Not only that, when my father passed away many years later, I discovered that what I remembered about my Grandpa Aaron was seen from my mother's womb. When my family would have gatherings and someone would bring up Grandpa Aaron's name, I told the story of what I remembered about him. I would always tell of the incident about how he tried to hit me and my mom with his stick. I actually remembered this so vividly. I can see it now even as I am writing this. I remembered which room in the house it was, and some details as to the reason why he was hitting at me and my mom. I thought that I just happened to be in the room with my mom and he tried to hit me because I was there. He was so mean to my mom.

On the day of my father's burial, after his body was committed into the grave, I was looking at the headstones of other relatives and I saw grandpa Aaron's grave and headstone. I saw that he had passed away in November, 1958. I was in awe because I was born in March of 1959. Wow! How could I have seen this?

I was in my mother's womb. No one else was in the room. Wow! I really saw the bond between my mom and me. I dealt with fear in my life and I see where it got its roots In Jeremiah 1:5 God says, "Before I formed you in the womb, I knew you; before you were born, I sanctified you; and I ordained you a prophet to the nations." There are two other events in my childhood that let me know that I am in the Kingdom of God for such a time as this. We must Follow the purpose even in our pain. The purpose will bring you through the pain.

A few years back, one of the ladies who grew up in our community was visiting my sister, Annette. She told me, "You were a pretty baby." She also told me that she remembered when I was an infant and that my dad had knocked me out of my mother's arms and I was hospitalized for a while. As she was telling me this, my other sister Helen just happened to be there and joined in on the conversation and she said "Yes, this is true." She remembered it as well. Up until that point, I had no idea that I had been hospitalized as an infant because of my father's abusiveness.

As the conversation went on my sisters told me also that when I was a little girl, I almost was run over by a big truck; how I almost drowned as I was being carried downstream in the creek; and how I was also stuck in a culvert and my other sister pulled me out with a fishing hook. I have the scar today from that one. Wow! God brought me through all that and into the Kingdom of God for such a time as this.

Those attacks seemed to have been physical attacks, but those attacks formed scars deep on the inside; and those scars on the inside were the ones which brought about the most pain, heartache, grief, unforgiveness, bitterness, hatred, anger, and confusion. I know that it was God who had His hand on my life and preserved me through it all.

In spite of the pain, the purpose will prevail, if you don't quit. I remember being so sad after that horrible event when my mother got killed. It happened in February of that year. I was in the eighth grade; my life was shattered, and I had no idea that there would be purpose in my pain.

When I got a job and my own place, I began to reach out to my nieces and nephews and other children in my community. I would bake cookies, and would often feed them a meal. I even started a youth Bible study in my home. I had compassion for children because of the pain I had suffered as a child. I was really misguided concerning relationships. I felt that I didn't deserve a good man in my life. I was told things like, "You better get that man; he's got a job." Because of what I had seen exemplified before me in my father, I thought that I had to settle. I felt that if I got someone who wouldn't beat upon me, I would be ok. I was wrong. Although, I had determined that I would not get one that would beat me like I had seen happen to my mom. I did enter into a relationship without the guidance of the Lord and it was not good. He ended up choking me one night. You will attract what you think you deserve, even though that is not what you want.

Every time that I look back over my life I see the hand of God: how He walked me through the pain, hatred, anger, bitterness and unforgiveness. He healed me and I found my purpose in the pain. I want my readers to know that healing, deliverance, and freedom is possible, and remember that Love never fails.

Forgiveness will emerge. Hatred will turn to compassion. Fear will leave as you build faith in God. Failure will be turned into success. Low self esteem will turn into an attitude of, *I can*. Lack will turn into prosperity. I see now that anger, hatred and unforgiveness had me locked in, and I couldn't succeed.

Today I mentor young women, and pastor alongside my husband, and we together minister hope, healing and entrepreneurship to many. God intends for the whole man to prosper.

My husband and I have multiple businesses; and together we are helping to build the kingdom of God and changing the world one life at a time. I want to encourage those who can't seem to do better but want to, and encourage those who don't know how to get there, or think that they can't. Remember the Scripture tells us in Philippians 4:13, "I can do all things through Christ Who strengthens me."

Because of the pain, empathy arises for the hurting and the purpose to bring healing to the hurting is fulfilled. Don't quit. You will find purpose even in the pain that you are experiencing right now. Healing is for you, and Love never fails.

I have been brought to the Kingdom of God for such a time as this to let you know that you can be delivered and live a fulfilled life. I have a mandate from God to share my testimony of deliverance and healing in this book to bring others into their place of purpose in spite of the pain. The Lord delivered me from self-destruction. The wound was so deep, but The Love that Mama taught me went deeper than the wound. Healing is possible for you. Love never fails. You can do it!

Tips and tool:

Are you thinking, thoughts like: Why am I here in this place? How did I get here?

I didn't do anything wrong, but wrong had invaded my life. I didn't know the scar was so deep. Will I ever get over this? Is it possible for me to be delivered and set free?

Answers:

Yes, you can do all things through Christ who strengthens you. Strength with your deliverance is available.

- Pray and ask the Lord to lead you to someone who you can confide in—someone who will just listen to your story. Pouring out is a dose of healing in itself.

- Get a pen and paper and write down how and what you are feeling right now.

When we keep *trouble* bound up on the inside of us, it can become explosive and detrimental to our mental, emotional, and physical health.

"I have a calm and undisturbed mind and heart and it is the life and health of my body…" (Proverbs 14:30 AMPC)

DAILY CONFESSIONS:

- I have a calm and undisturbed mind and heart (Proverbs 14:30 AMPC).

- I can do all things through Christ who strengthens me (Phil 4:13).

- God is my strength and power and maketh my way perfect (2 Sam 22:32 KJV).

- Love never fails me (1 Cor 13:8 NIV).

- My heart is not troubled (disturbed) (John 14:1).

- My heart is no longer broken, it is fixed trusting in the Lord (Ps 112:7 NKJV).

- The Greater One lives on the inside of me (1 John 4:4 KJV).

- I don't worry or be anxious about anything anymore (Phil 4:6 NKJV).

This is a self-help book, written to bring healing to you as you navigate through the situations that have caused pain in your life, to bring you to your purpose, even in your pain. You are not the only one who has needed help in these areas.

Now, you must make the decision to get up and practice these self-help tools in this book. These tools were inspired by God. You can find purpose in your pain.

"…His favor is for life; Weeping may endure for a night, but joy comes in the morning" (Psalm 30:5 NKJV).

Notes

_____
_____
_____
_____
_____
_____
_____
_____
_____
_____
_____
_____
_____
_____
_____
_____
_____
_____
_____
_____
_____
_____
_____
_____
_____

CHAPTER 8

"Living Beyond The Loss"

There is a difference in living and existing. Living is to have the power to continue running, flowing, or producing action. It is animation and vigor to spring forward. The Hebrew word *chayah* and the Greek word *Zao* are the primary terms for life in the Bible.

Chayah is a verb that means to live; to have life; to continue to live.

Zao, is translated as "living" in the New Testament. The word exist, (in this sense), means: to stay alive; survive; to have been, or reality; living by breathing; to eke out a living; (eke – To obtain or create, but just barely, in other words to scrap or scrape).

Acts 17:28 says, "For in Him we live and move and have our being."

In Christ we will have the power to continue and spring forward, producing action; we can flow and have vigor, and in all of this we exist. We are here in Him and because of Him. I want you to really see the difference between the two words. As we go from day to day in this life, we are either living or just existing.

Life is too precious to just exist—to eke out a living (barely live, to scrape).

After the loss of my mom I believe that I was just existing. I had no hope of moving forward, or being productive. I couldn't see myself being successful or doing meaningful things in life without my mom. I only wanted to exist (eke out some life), so that someday I could help my younger siblings. I had believed that because of what happened to my mom, I would automatically fail. I had no desire to excel in life and I had no one to give me that push to do my best, even though I desired instructions. During school for the few years that followed, I just simply existed (eked). Some of my friends in school were not interested in going higher in life. So, I didn't even try to get good grades because I wanted to fit in. I was once an honor roll student, and enjoyed making good grades. I enjoyed bringing my little green report card home to my parents. I would receive achievement certificates in different areas of academics.

After the loss of my mom, I only dreamed that someday things would get better, but I had no producing actions—no zeal—no drive. In school I was just existing. I really just looked forward to lunch time. I lived in deep grief, pain, sorrow, and anger daily. There is no life in grief, only hopelessness. At home I would slip away and read my Bible. I didn't want any of my siblings to catch me reading, so I would hide. You see, The Bible was no stranger to any of us children, especially my sister and I who were next to each other in age. You see, my dad (before he killed my mom), would get drunk—down drunk and call for my sister and me to get the Bible and read it to him. When we began to read he would quote the Scriptures as we read them. Wow! How did he know those Scriptures?

He once told me that when he was a little boy (after his mom died prematurely), he would get his Bible and go out under a tree and read it. I realized later that even though my dad was drunk when he made us read the Bible to him, *life* was entering us from the Word. Even though the Bible was no stranger to us, some of my siblings would still make fun of me. They would call me Miss Nun as I mentioned before. After my mom was killed, no one in the house went to church except for maybe Easter or Christmas. My mom was an usher at the church. She was brought up in church and brought us up in church. I still have the picture of my mom in her usher uniform. The more I thought about the way things used to be before the loss of my mom, it only made me angrier and sadder. I was just existing—dwelling in the pit of anger, regret, bitterness, grief, hatred, and unforgiveness—just barely making it. We were in deep poverty—same old same old every day—no hope for tomorrow. At that time, my only ambition was to try to help my three younger siblings, and that was it. I felt like I owed it to my mom to see about her little ones. The mentality of just existing, barely making it from one day to the next was constant. However, I always had this desire tucked away in me to connect to the Lord. As I mentioned in one of the previous chapters, I didn't understand it, but there was a war going on inside of me. The "Get up and do better" attitude was warring against the "You will never come out of this place, this pit, so don't even try" attitude. I remember making up my mind one day to go back to church. I had no transportation to take me to church. I was only 14 years old and none of my siblings were interested in going to church at that time. "She's the one that goes to church," was the label given to me by some of my siblings.

I used to see my neighbor, Mrs. Jackson, walking to church when she didn't have transportation. One day, I asked if I could ride with her, and she gladly said yes. As a teenager, I would even hitchhike to church—no one told me to go, no one forced me. There was a deep yearning inside me, calling me out of that pit. I am so grateful that I chose to live again—living in the Word.

On days when Mrs. Jackson didn't have a ride, we walked to church together. Even under the sweltering heat, we kept moving, determined to make it to service. Mrs. Jackson, though sometimes weary, never let exhaustion stop her. She walked on, sweating off her makeup, but nothing deterred her from reaching the church. Much blessing is stored up for Mrs. Jackson, who took the time to help me rise beyond my loss.

I began to get vigor, and spring forward again. Even though I was still wrestling with the hatred, anger, bitterness, and resentment, I was, however, producing some positive steps.

The story of the four lepers, in the Bible, tells that they made a decision to get up. They said, "Why sit we here and die?" I can recall one day when I was so hungry and we didn't have any food. We lived in the countryside. I remember walking up the highway to the store which was about a mile and a quarter away. I had no money, but I asked Mr. Robert, who was the owner of the store, if he would let me have some food on credit. After some hesitation, He said, yes. I don't remember all that I bought that day, but I was so glad to get some food and headed straight home. I don't remember, but I am sure that I ate some of it before I got back home. I brought food back for us all. I became a provider that day, and was living beyond the loss. At some point, I got a summer job at the local college cafeteria through a summer program for children and I got paid every two weeks. God alone helped me get to and from work each day. When I got my check (which wasn't much), about $44.00, I took it home and gave it to my sister who was taking care of us, to spend in the household for whatever was needed. I enjoyed work. I was beginning to live again and not just exist. I began to live beyond the loss but that was only the beginning.

That may not have seemed like big steps, but healing was taking place, and I began to see that there was life beyond the greatest loss in my life. Healing was a process—year by year—step by step, I began to live beyond the loss. Healing is like a cabbage or an onion. It comes in layers. My healing process began, and I didn't realize that it was taking place.

Healing is truly a lifelong journey, but it gets easier over time. What I mean by this is that God heals and it is a done deal, but staying healed from the vices is the journey. Love never fails. Even though I had low self-esteem, I would still hope for that brighter day. I begin to dream again of coming out of that dark pit.

I got involved in the school band and I enjoyed that—trying to Live beyond the loss, even though I still felt so lost without the guidance of my mom. I would still visit the cemetery as often as I could throughout the process of grieving. Grief was still poisoning me and I didn't know it. The Lord delivered me from the grief, pain, loneliness, and the constant focusing on the great loss. He let me know that I could live again and not just exist, or survive. Yes, I did survive, but What is beyond survival. You want to go beyond survival, because survival is a miserable life. You must get what you need to sustain you for life and living. I believe that if the Lord had not had His hand on my life, I would not be here writing this book of encouragement. This is a survivor's story for you.

Remember, survivors live to tell their stories. Acts 17:28 (KJV) says, "For in Him we live, and move, and have our being…There is life after the loss.

Tips and tools:

- Know that the *loss* is not bigger than the One who gave the gift in the first place.
- Don't let your mind return to the place where it was hurt.

Isaiah 26:3 (KJV) says, "He will keep him in perfect peace whose mind is stayed on Him…"

- If the memory hurts, stay away from it. Dismiss it, in Jesus' name.

- Make new traditions on those special days that you once celebrated with that one who is no longer with you.

It's not over and you might not see it right now, but your latter can be greater. HAGGAI 2:9 (KJV) says "The glory of this latter house shall be greater than of the former', saith the LORD of hosts. 'And in this place will I give peace,' saith the LORD of hosts." Remember that Jesus bore your grief and carried your sorrows for you.

Jeremiah 29:11 (one of my favorite scriptures), lets me know that God is the giver of life, and He has a future and a hope for me and for you. Philippians 4:8 (KJV) says, "Finally, brethren, whatsoever things are true, whatsoever things are honest, whatsoever things are just, whatsoever things are pure, whatsoever things are lovely, whatsoever things are of good report; if there be any virtue, and if there be any praise, think on these things." Life is good because it came from God, and you can live a victorious life after the loss! I have a fulfilled life of hope and love. It has been and is a journey.

The tragic loss of my mother is not the only loss or betrayal of a loved one, or even sickness that I have had to journey through, but He (God) sent His Word which healed and delivered me from my destruction. Thank God! I was on the road to self-destruction. The Lord gave me Jeremiah 30:17 years ago. I had never read it before that time. The Lord just took me to it, and it says, "For I, God will restore health unto you and heal you of your wounds..."

The Lord was letting me know that He had already "got" the situation before I even knew what trial He was about to walk me through. That was years after my mom was killed, and another situation which concerned my health. The scripture, when believed and claimed, works for all pain: including heartaches, anger, and bitterness. That sickness, loss, betrayal, and the rest of evils didn't come from God, but He walked me through it. He is the healer of it all.

Confessions:

- Healing is possible for me, and I receive it.
- There is life beyond this loss for me and I receive it!
- I will live and not die and declare the works (goodness) of the Lord; and I receive that Word, in Jesus' name!
- Love (God) will never fail me; and I receive it.

Receive in the Greek is Lambano which means—to take it, lay hold of it. So, lay hold of your healing so you can live beyond the loss. Healing is for you and you can live beyond the loss. According to 1 Timothy 6:17, He gives us all things richly to enjoy and that includes life beyond the loss: whether that be because of the death of a loved one through tragedy, divorce, or betrayal. Whatever the situation, you can live beyond the loss. Isaiah 26:3 says, "Thou wilt keep him in perfect peace, whose mind is stayed on thee: because he trusteth in thee." Healing is for you and " Love never fails."

What are you feeling now?

Write it down:

Notes

_____
_____
_____
_____
_____
_____
_____
_____
_____
_____
_____
_____
_____
_____
_____
_____
_____
_____
_____
_____
_____
_____
_____
_____
_____

CHAPTER 9

A Message Of Hope

Like me, you may have had the horrific experience of a parent who took the life of the other parent; or someone else may have taken the life of a parent, or someone else that's near and dear to you. You may have gone through a bad relationship in marriage, or even a divorce. You may have had an unfaithful spouse who betrayed your trust, and broke confidence. All of these scenarios can produce anger, hatred, bitterness, fear, confusion, and unforgiveness.

I know that you may have been treated unfairly or unjustly, but healing is available for you. Your healing and deliverance are not depending on that person who hurt you. Healing from these kinds of hurt just doesn't happen automatically. You must want it, and do whatever is necessary to get it. I have shared parts of my story with many people who have struggled with bitterness, unforgiveness, anger and grief; whether it be because of the loss of a loved one, a divorce, betrayal, or broken relationships. The message that love never fails, and that there is life after the loss, has been a great healing tool. I had to claim and receive healing in order for the purpose to come forth out of what was a shattered life for me. I am glad that the Lord healed me and brought me into His kingdom for such a time as this.

There is purpose on the other side of this. Our main purpose is as found in Ecclesiastes 12:13, "Let us hear the conclusion of the whole matter: Fear God, and keep his commandments: for this is the whole duty of man." The whole duty of man is to serve God then He will purposefully give you your assignment in life. In the book of Ruth, Boaz left Ruth's hands full of purpose. God will give you your purpose, (your assignment) Amen! Your latter shall be greater!

"The glory of this latter house shall be greater than of the former, saith the LORD of hosts…"(Haggai 2:9)

Your pain is real, but it does not have to define your future. Consider what Jeremiah 29:11 (NIV) says, "For I know the plans I have for you," declares the LORD, "plans to prosper you and not to harm you, plans to give you hope and a future." Healing is possible, and it is for you, today. You are not alone.

He sent His Word to heal you and deliver you from all the destruction that the enemy has plotted against you.

I have said over and over in this book that love never fails. I had to come to the reality that I had no capability on my own to receive healing from the grief, hatred, anger, unforgiveness, bitterness and resentment that had infested me; and that I could only love through God. I also had to come to the realization that no good thing dwells in the flesh: "For I know that in me (that is, in my flesh) dwelleth no good thing; for to will is present with me; but how to perform that which is good, I find not" (Romans 7:18).

Just a bit of humor here: When we were growing up, my mom bought our first family TV set. One summer evening (it was still daylight outside) a man named, Woodie was telling the weather and all of a sudden, bow-yah! My dad came in drunk, threw a thick glass-Coke bottle and burst the TV set. WOW! It puffed smoke.

It felt like someone had died around our house. All of a sudden there was no life where the TV was sitting. I had to let God love him through me, because I hated him even back then for being so mean to us. I didn't realize that hatred could accelerate to such a high level, until after my dad killed my mom. I can laugh about him shattering the TV now. God is really a restorer of life. Years later, the Lord has blessed me with a seven-bedroom house and there is a TV in all of them except for one, and that is by choice. I tell you of this incident to prove to you that life can be fulfilling even after the loss. Loss is loss. Pick up the pieces and live.

Tips and tools:

Take these steps towards your healing process:

1. First of all, you must believe in your innermost being, that Love (which is God) will never fail.

2. Acknowledge that grief is too big for you alone and that it is a killer.

3. Acknowledge that hatred is too much for you. It is a destroyer, and that it destroys the giver more than the one it is aimed at.

4. Acknowledge that anger is too massive and destructive for you alone, and it will cause you to do foolish things that you may regret. The Bible says that anger rests (abides in, is at home and comfortable) in the bosom of fools. Anger could cause physical illnesses to come upon your body. It is a killer.

5. Acknowledge that unforgiveness seals your own fate, and could be fatal. Mark 11:26 says, "But if ye do not forgive, neither will your Father which is in heaven forgive your trespasses".

6. Acknowledge that your own forgiveness is blocked when you don't forgive. (I was blocking my own forgiveness when I refused to forgive my dad). Unforgiveness causes you to carry that one who caused the pain and hurt everywhere you go. You are allowing them to dictate your life and future, and that's too much for you to bear on your own.

7. Acknowledge that bitterness is bitter and never sweet. Hebrews 12:15 (KJV) says, "Looking diligently lest any man fail of the grace of God; lest any root of bitterness spring up to trouble you, and thereby many be defiled…" Bitterness will grow deep and strong in you, and it is too much for the natural man to bear. Bitterness can take root, grow, and bring forth fruits of defilement (a state of being unclean, dishonored, desecrated) for oneself and affecting others.

8. Acknowledge that resentment is a burden you don't want to bear. It is a negative reaction to an event that is perceived as unfair or unjust. It is a weak, passive emotion. Resentment turns into bitterness, anger, spite, and hatred. This is too much for the human mind (soul). All of this is handled through the soul when you are dealing with it on your own.

Notes

CHAPTER 10

Walking Out Your Healing

In the previous chapter, I mentioned that I cried out to the Lord and told him that I couldn't love my dad; and His response was, "No, you can't love him in yourself or on your own, but through Me you can." When you start loving the one that you hated you will know that something supernatural took place. God is doing the loving, forgiving, and the releasing, through you. You are only the conduit.

POINTS OF HEALINGS

Stop thinking that:

- I can't ever forgive.
- I can't be cordial toward him/her or them.
- I will always resent him/her or them.
- I will always be angry with him/her or them for what he/she or they have done to me.
- I hate him/her or them.

If you are saying or thinking about anything that is mentioned above, these things are coming from your soul: your mind, will, and emotions; not your spirit.

CONFESSIONS (Make these confessions daily)

- Confess Phil 4:13: I can do all things through Christ who strengthens me. Look at what it says—through Christ—not I, myself can do all things. Through Christ, I can be the conduit that loves.

- Through Christ, I can be the conduit that forgives.

- Through Christ, I can be the conduit that releases that one who inflicted this pain, grief, and hurt upon me.

- Healing is possible for me, only through Christ. Isaiah 26:3 says, "He will keep him in perfect peace whose mind is stayed on thee."

I know that the video of what happened keeps on playing over and over in your mind; but if something that you don't want to see comes on the television, you just simply get the remote and change the channel. If you keep meditating on those mental videos of the incident , you will revert to the anger. If you meditate on the mental video of what they did to you, it will keep the relational bonds broken. If you meditate on that video of what he/she, or they did, and how they did what they did, you will remain in bondage—in rage. Rage is only anger, bitterness, hatred, and unforgiveness unleashed; it is too much for your natural man. It will cause an explosion inside of you if left alone and not dealt with. It could affect your physical and mental health. It could also affect you relationally. No one wants to be around a person who is angry and bitter all the time.

The first step to real life is to accept Jesus as Lord and Savior. Surrender your life to Him for He knows what you are wrestling with. He knows the pain and discontentment. Even though He knows, just take the time to tell Him.

Prayer

"Lord, I feel _____

_____

_____

_____

_____

_____

_____

_____

_____

and I can't handle this on my own. I surrender my heart and all my problems to you. I confess with my mouth the Lord Jesus, and I believe in my heart that God you have raised Jesus from the dead, and I am saved. Amen!

I want to live and not just exist after this loss that I am having to deal with. As the scripture says, "We (I) don't know what to do, but our (my) eyes are upon you. The battle is not yours (mine), but it is the Lord's."

Read: Romans 10:9,10; John 3:16; John 10:10; Ps 107:20

Healing, forgiveness, and love are all available for you to reach out by faith and claim, in Jesus' name .

The Love that Mama talked about will never fail. Even though my mom was gone from this side, her message still had life, and that *life* brought me out of and from spiritual death.

Your words are powerful. Hebrews 11:3 tells us that the worlds were framed by the Word of God. It is important that you call only what you want into existence— not things that you don't want.

1 PETER 3:10 NKJV: "For he that would love life and see good days, let him refrain his tongue from evil, and his lips that they speak no guile…"

Guile – deceit, cunning, or craftiness. It's often used to describe words or actions that are insincere.

Refrain –to hold back, to abstain.

PSALM 103:20 (KJV) SAYS, "Bless the LORD, ye His angels that excel in strength, that do His commandments, hearkening unto the voice of His word."

Angels hearken (pay attention to, obey and comply with) to the voice of God's Words. They don't hearken to feelings.

We must speak the Word of God, not our own words based on how we feel, and angels will listen and obey God's Word that is coming out of your mouth.

Are you a part of a local church family? If not, I encourage you to ask God to lead you to that church family that is a perfect fit for you. When seeking for a church family, don't go looking for perfection from the people, but go looking for the Lord who is perfect in all His ways. A good church should be a place of integrity and is Word based. It should be a place of teaching. If you are a part of a local church family, and it meets all of the right criteria, I encourage you to get more involved. Learn and absorb as much as you can when the Word is going forth.

Be a blessing to your church family. When you really look closer you may find others there who are dealing with losses greater than yours. The Bible says, "He that waters shall be watered." So, be a help to others.

Tips and tools

Journaling also is very important

- Do you feel like some days you can't even put words to what you are feeling?
- Does your wound feel so deep that you can't get a hold on it?
- Have you stopped dreaming?

Find the Answers to these questions in the Word of God, write them down and expect the answers to be manifested in your life.

You should also get connected to a Word-based support group in your area or through media. Here are a few resources:

- Dr. Shanicka N. Scarbrough, MD (www.DrShanicka.org)
- Rachel L. Thompson — Healing Room Ministry https://rachellthompson.com
- The Healing Package Daily Reading (By Rachel Thompson)

"So if the Son sets you free, you will be free indeed." John 8:36

Notes

Biography

Rachel Thompson – Pastor | Speaker | Author | Entrepreneur

Rachel Thompson is a dedicated pastor, speaker, author, and entrepreneur with over 30 years of ministry experience. Alongside her husband, Vester, she co-founded The House of Refuge Intl. Church in Prentiss, Mississippi, where she has passionately taught faith, healing, and prosperity with clarity and conviction.

She is a graduate of Prentiss High School and Geiger Beauty/Cosmetology School. Rachel became an entrepreneur at the age of 23 and has since built a thriving career. She has successfully launched and managed multiple businesses, including Sassy Scissors Beauty Salon and Supply, V&R Trucking, and Rachel's Dispatching Service. As a business coach, she has helped others establish trucking and brokerage companies across various states.

Committed to community service, Rachel co-founded Raisola Park, a seven-acre recreational space honoring her late mother. The park has hosted numerous events, including regional gatherings for individuals with special needs, back-to-school programs, and law enforcement appreciation days.

As an author, Rachel has written The Encourager newsletter, The Healing Package, and Set Free, a book focused on overcoming grief, bitterness, and unforgiveness. She also leads The Healing Room

Ministry, providing spiritual and emotional restoration through prayer and teaching.

Rachel is deeply committed to serving others, volunteering at food pantries and nursing homes, and offering encouragement and faith-based guidance. She serves as a prayer coach, leading Saturday morning prayer sessions to teach effective prayer.

Recognized for her entrepreneurial success, Rachel and her husband were honored with the Entrepreneur of the Year award from the Jefferson Davis County Chamber of Commerce. Under the spiritual covering of Kenneth Copeland Ministries, they continue to expand their ministry and business ventures, empowering others through faith, leadership, and service.

Raisola Park

(The story behind Raisola Park)

Raisola Park came into being through a vision from God given to my husband Pastor, Vester Thompson. The Lord spoke to him and told him to build a park and to name it Raisola Park in honor of my mother, Raisola Harrien Bryant, who was killed at the hand of my dad through domestic violence. She left 10 adolescent and adult children behind. The Lord spoke to Pastor Vester and told him that, *where innocent blood was shed, God would get vengeance.* This means that Raisola Park would be a safe haven for children to come, play and be blessed. Families can gather and celebrate reunions, birthdays and many other family-friendly events.

Raisola Park grounds consist of seven beautiful acres with custom-built park and play equipment including grills, water slides, a family friendly pavilion with rocking chairs and hammocks for relaxation, and much more.

Raisola Park is the place where Pastor Vester and I, and The House of Refuge host many community events such as, special needs children and adult-fun days, Pastors and Law Enforcement Day, Family Fest, Regional back to school events, birthdays, special meetings, conferences and much more. Rosa, Lydia (Ann) Charles (Charlie Boy), Annette, Willie Booth, Perry Bryant (Siblings) were major contributors in helping

Pastor Vester and me to bring Raisola Park into existence. Others in the family unit were vital supporters as well.

Special thanks to my uncle, Bill C. Harrien (my mom's brother). He and my mom were very close. Special thanks to his children, (Fannie and Al Brown, L.B. Harrien, Bill and Valerie Harrien, and Eddie Harrien—all who partnered with us to make Raisola Park a reality. Special thanks to all the Chicago family who contributed in any way.

A very special thanks to The House of Refuge Intl. Church. As a result of their input and contributions people have come from all across the United States to events at Raisola Park.

If tragedy happens in a family, work to strengthen that which remains.

"Be watchful and strengthen the things which remain... Rev 3:2"

Out of the tragedy came RAISOLA PARK.